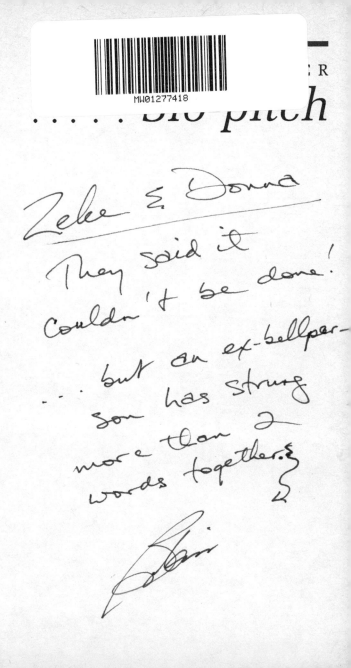

ER

...... big pitch

Zeke & Donna

They said it
couldn't be done!

... but an ex-bellper-
son has strung
more than 2
words together.
}

PLAY BETTER
..... *Slo-pitch*

Dan Osborne
Blair Tullis

SUMMERHILL PRESS, *Toronto*

© 1990   Dan Osborne and Blair Tullis

Published by
Summerhill Press
52 Shaftesbury Ave,
Toronto, ON M4T 1A2

Distributed by
University of Toronto Press
5201 Dufferin Street
Downsview, ON M3H 5T8

Illustrations by Laurie Lafrance
Design concept by Karen Klett

Printed and bound in Canada

Ist edition

**Canadian Cataloguing in Publication Data**
Osborne, Dan, 1945-
        Play better slo-pitch
ISBN 0-929091-20-5
1. Slow pitch softball.
I. Tullis, Blair, 1946-    II. Title.
GV881.08 1990    796.357'8    C90-093692-4

To Ginny, Sue, Alison,
Cam, Stephanie and Tyler.
Great families...great fans.

# • • • • • *Contents*

# Introduction

There have been a lot of books published about baseball since the first edition of *Batting and Pitching* appeared in 1884. Everyone from managers to pitchers have had a go at the game. So why, you may ask, do we need another one?

Well, considering that slo-pitch softball is North America's fastest growing team sport, with over 40 million players on the continent, someone had to aim a book straight at those who could use a little help to elevate the level of their game.

Played by men and women of every age, shape and size, slo-pitch has brought people from all walks of life back to the diamond for two reasons: to have a good time, and to get some exercise.

Slo-pitch, by its very nature, is designed for those who put the fun side of the game first. It's a game of hitting, running and fielding action where pitchers scrape the clouds trying to throw you the perfect home run ball. Everyone gets involved in the play, so there are lots of opportunities to shine...or to mess up.

Whatever drives your particular team — winning at any cost or just enjoying the fact that you're wearing a real baseball sweater — everyone has the desire to play well. How often, however, have you seen your team give up needless runs because someone didn't know the basics? Up until now, there has been no source of information available to help slo-pitch players to think in the right direction. That is why we have decided to put together this book for you.

So where do two slightly paunchy, yet still cunning, players get their information? As well as trusting our playing and managing experience, we read every instructional manual on baseball and soft-ball that we could lay our hands on, reviewed instructional videos and watched a lot of very good tournament teams in action. Most important, however, we talked to the people who play the sport. We got tips from players who are serious, players who are talented and players who know how to have a good time

• • • • •   — all of them lovers of the game.
They told us about the quirks and the
fine points, and about the fundamen-
tals they wish they had learned
sooner.

What we've ended up with is a
distillation of softball playing information as it relates to slo-pitch. It
contains tips that can help you to
become more aware of game situations, play to the best of your abilities and have fun in the process.
There are tips on hitting, pitching,
baserunning, fielding, coaching and
more — we can even help you to get
your body as ready to play as it will
ever be.

You'll learn how to relax and get
back to basics, even when you're 0
for 3 and one pitch away from buy-
ing the beer for the third week in a
row.

This is not an instruction manual,
and you won't find involved discus-
sions of the rules or management
styles. But no matter what your level
of play, you'll find thought-provok-
ing ideas, new insights and gentle
reminders. Some will make you

chuckle; others will cause a knowing • • • • •
nod. You may even get a groan or
two, remembering a bonehead move
or a botched play.

So read on, have some fun, and
*Play Better Slo-Pitch.*

# 1 Hitting

Well, why not? Everyone loves this part of the game. We can't wait to get to the plate. We want to look cool (and twenty pounds lighter), intimidate the pitcher, and convince ourselves that we should have been put at the top of the order. We dream of hitting one over the fence, yet feel lucky to end up safe on first base.

It's at the plate where we meet our moment of truth. We look silly or macho, frightened or confident — and always slightly out of shape. More to the point, this is where all our skills and concentration must come into play at once, with an instinct borne of practice and going over the basics, mentally, again and again.

Here are some tips to increase your effectiveness in the batter's box.

CHOOSING
A BAT

Not everyone can hit the ball over the fence. Many of us like to think of ourselves as spray hitters — able to hit the ball to all fields — but in our more honest moments we have to admit that we are usually surprised at where the ball ends up. Here are some ways in which the choice of a bat can increase your control, helping you to place the ball with something more than luck.

• Don't be influenced by what the bat looks like when it's new. The sexiest-looking bat will become grungy after a few games unless you don't hit anything. Worry about how it feels.

• Aluminum bats carry the ball farther and faster than wooden bats.

• A bat weighted towards the head of the barrel gives you a better chance at hitting the ball over the fence, but sacrifices some wrist control.

• A bottle bat (one with a longer barrel) gives you a better chance to make contact with the ball. The even balance, however, makes it less attractive for the long ball hitter.

• A light, evenly balanced bat maximizes wrist control. It's your wrist that aims singles all over the park.

• The thickness of the grip makes no difference to the flight of the

• • • • • ball. Just choose one that feels comfortable in your hands.

• Bats come in a wide variety of weights. Again, choose the one that feels good and that you can control with ease.

THE GRIP   Here's where you can really look like a pro: it's all in the gloves. Gloves are not merely decorative. They protect your hands from blisters, improve your grip when your hands sweat (in hot weather or when you're in a slump), and cushion a blow, particularly in cold weather when a ball hit off the wrong part of the bat feels like an electric shock up your arm. Obviously, a thin glove allows you to feel the bat in your hands more than a thick glove. Although some prefer to wear two gloves, most wear a glove only on the lower hand (left hand on a right handed hitter).

However, as with all the important things of life there are two schools of thought on gloves. One says you replace your batting gloves frequently so they always look new. Hey, if it works for Dave Winfield,

how can you say no? The other
school says, let 'em get grubby.
People will know you've done this
batting thing a lot. So if you're of the
first school, pass along your used
batting gloves to someone of the
second. Then both of you can get
down to work:

- How you grip the bat is up to you.
  However, conventional wisdom
  has it that the bat should lie along
  the base of the fingers rather than
  along the palms.

- Line up your knuckles so that the
  base of the fingers of the upper
  hand align with the middle of the
  fingers of the lower hand. (Sounds

*Line up your knuckles*

- silly but it works) This is the most common grip.
- If you tend to hit too many fly balls, a change in your grip may correct the problem. Instead of aligning your fingers, line up your knuckles. This will bring the back elbow up and flatten the curve of your swing.

*Bring the back elbow up*

- Grip the bat firmly, but not too tight — flexible but firm. If your grip is too loose, you lose control of the bat. If it is too tight you will be less able to flex your wrists and swing smoothly.

- Avoid using a reverse grip, e.g., batting right-handed with the left hand above the right. It looks sexy but usually disappoints. You lose follow-through and power and increase your risk of injury.

- Macho hitters claim that choking up on the bat, that is gripping the bat higher on the neck, is wimpish. It isn't. It increases your bat control, although it restricts your hitting distance. Unless you can hit it out of the park every time, don't let would-be sluggers inhibit you: choke up on that bat, if it feels right! After all, choking up on the bat to get a hit beats choking at the plate.

## THE STANCE

Now that you and the bat are one, here's how and where to stand in the batter's box in order to let the bat do its stuff.

- Relax! (Easy for us to say when you're the one who's up to bat. We sympathize.) Hitting can be a matter of luck or discipline. If you don't want to wait on luck, you'll need rhythm, balance and full extension of the arms over the plate.

- - - - - None of these are possible unless you're relaxed.

- Keep your weight balanced on the balls of your feet.

- Bend slightly at the waist. Your knees should feel slightly soft — poised but not locked. If you crouch too low, you will swing up rather than flat across, resulting in high fly balls rather than lower driving hits.

- Stand near the back of the box. This forces you to take the time to watch the ball come in over the plate. Standing level with the plate tempts you to swing early (and high), before the ball drops into the strike zone.

- Keep the back foot firmly on the ground throughout the swing. This will give your swing more power.

- For the best combination of power and balance, keep your feet shoulder-width apart.

- When you hit the ball, your arms should be stretched out their full length. If you are too close to the plate, move farther back in the box to allow for this complete extension. A swing that is too tight will sacrifice power.

- There are three basic stances at the plate:

(a) the **square** stance:

Both feet are about the same distance from the plate. This stance tends to produce hits that go straight down the middle of the field. It allows good control and moderate power.

(b) the **closed** stance:

The front foot is closer to the plate than is the back foot. This stance can increase power but

limits flexibility. Use this stance to hit to the opposite field.

(c) the **open** stance:

The back foot is closer to the plate than is the front foot. In this stance you can place the ball most easily, pull hitting down the line or spraying hits to all fields. However, you'll generate less power than with a closed stance.

Now that you have the basic stances down cold, you need to think about the mechanics of hitting. One of the elements that often gets less attention than it should is the way you stride into the ball.

- Start your stride just before your swing. The forward movement gets your momentum going.

- Don't lunge at the ball. You'll lose control of the swing and mishit the ball. A smooth, controlled swing is the key.

- Don't make your stride too long or you will lose power.

- Begin your stride with your weight on your back foot. During your stride, shift your weight to the front foot. (If you begin your swing with your weight already on your front foot, you will get no power from the movement of your body: only your arms will be powering the ball.)

**THE ANGLE OF THE SWING**

You're positioned properly in the box, confident you can hit this one over the fence. Here it comes, the perfect pitch. So, why is your bat suddenly transformed into an axe or a golf club? Here's how to swing it properly

- Be patient. Well, behave as if you were patient. Let the ball come to you. When it does, make sure it's a pitch you want before going for it.

- As you begin to swing, move the bat back first, then forward. This sets up a pendulum motion in the bat, building speed and power as you shift your weight forward.

- Hold your hands and arms high. You'll feel the difference in flexibility.

- Keep your back elbow up to keep the bat from looping like a golf swing. A high elbow will help to keep your swing closer to the horizontal and will lessen the likelihood of hitting a high pop-up that is easy to field.

*Keep your back elbow up*

- The lower hand should dominate the swing. If the top hand is dominant, your wrists will roll forward and you will lose power.

- Move your hands sharply downward on the swing. This will ensure that your arms become completely extended and will help you hit more line drives.

*Move your hands sharply downward*

- Continue your swing through the ball and all the way around, releasing your top hand after contact, if necessary. A long, full swing will increase your power.

- The shoulder of your top hand should be facing the pitcher at the end of the swing. If it's there, you know that you have swung through properly.

- Make contact with the ball at the front of the plate with the hands flat. That means that a right-handed batter will have the fingertips of his right hand facing the sky on contact. Sounds weird, but look at your hands when you've hit a good one.

- Snap the wrists forward as your

bat hits the ball for maximum bat velocity. This wrist snap is what really makes the ball jump. If the wrists are not moving through and are trailing the bat, power is lost.

**THE HEAD**

The head should be used for more that just thinking. It also performs an important physical role. The head is the key to tracking the ball and controlling your swing.

- Always keep your head facing the pitcher, no matter what angle the rest of your body is at. Track the ball all the way from the pitcher's hand to your bat.

- Keep your head down right through the swing and the follow-through. As in golf, the head is the balance key that keeps all the elements of the swing together.

**GENERAL HITTING STRATEGY**

Granted, there are days when nothing will help; but after you've done nothing good at the plate, even sounding knowledgeable in the bar may help your self-esteem. These suggestions will help your game by getting back to the basics.

• • • • • • In the on-deck circle, focus your
mind as you loosen up your body.
Swing two bats or a weighted bat
(so it feels like you're swinging a
toothpick when you get to the
plate). Think about the general
game situation, so you can plan
how and where you want to hit
the ball to move runners, score
runs or just get on base.

• In the batter's box, relax and
think about the basics:

(a) position yourself in the box to
allow a fully extended swing;

(b) get balanced on the balls of
your feet;

(c) turn your face towards the
pitcher, ready to track the ball;

(d) relax.

• By the time you're up to bat, you
should have studied the pitcher:
what the pitcher has working
successfully; typical pitching
patterns? Is the pitcher having a
good outing? If not, let him or her
walk you. It may not be a flashy
way of getting on base, but it's
one for the team.

- Think positive. Think about where you want the hit to go, not just about getting a hit.

- Learning to switch hit is something best left to young kids who are either ambidextrous or indecisive. If you can't hit from both sides by now, forget it.

- All umpires decide on their own strike zone. It may have little to do with where you're standing, but you just have to live with whatever they decide. If umpires seem to be calling stikes that are deep, you may be too far up in the batter's box. Move back and give yourself a better chance of seeing the ball their way.

- Umpires often decide whether a pitch is a ball or a strike before it crosses the plate. This leaves them time to check the feet of the batter to make sure they stay in the batter's box.

- Don't be a selfish hitter: use the sacrifice fly to advance the runner. The game score is more important than your personal record.

• • • • • • Hit behind the runner. It takes practice but it keeps down the number of double plays and often advances the runner an extra base.

**PLACING THE BALL**

We all picture ourselves at batting practice hitting around the field at will — up the middle, down the lines, deep left and right. Nothing to it, right? Then we get up to bat and, truth is, we're usually grateful to make contact with the ball.

Somewhere in between lies a sensible course. You can develop a set of skills that will enable you to place the ball, i.e., direct the hit ball to a specific part of the field. Some of these suggestions contradict the general advice that we've already given: we're not inconsistent, hell no. It's just the old story: you have to know the rules before you can break them. What follows is the advanced course. Go ahead — break the rules!

• Think positively. Assume that you, rather than luck, control where the ball goes.

- An outside pitch is ideal for hitting to the opposite field. However, you can also effectively hit an inside pitch to the opposite field: take a step back and slap at the ball but don't follow through completely.

- Many hitters who can spray hits to all fields tend to stand even with the plate and hit the ball towards the front of the plate. Long ball hitters tend to stand back and wait for the ball to come to them.

- In order to push the ball to the opposite field, swing your hips around before your hands. The trailing hands will bring the bat head through later, pushing the ball to the opposite field.

- When using a closed stance place your feet slightly wider than shoulder width to gain power. You'll get greater distance on opposite field power hits.

# 2 *Baserunning*

Whether you slugged one or walked, there you are on base. Now, don't blow it: foolish mistakes can squander as many runs as smart baserunning can create. Mistakes on the basepaths not only ruin rallies, they do terrible things to team morale.

The keys to intelligent baserunning are straightforward: know the game situation and watch the coach, if there is one. (If not, listen to the most knowledgeable person screaming at you, as long as he or she is on your team.)

**WHAT EVERY BASERUNNER SHOULD KNOW**

Here are a few of the basics that should be kept in mind in baserunning situations. Follow these and the complicated stuff will take care of itself.

- Don't watch the ball you just hit. The split second you take to congratulate yourself may be the difference between being safe and being out. Let someone else tell you later how terrific your hit was. Then you can look genuinely surprised and please your public.

- On a single, turn either way when running through first base. It's always safer to turn away from the field, although most umpires will call you out only if it is clear that you were making an obvious attempt to get to second. Check your own league rules for variances, but remember that it's always safer to go the the right.

- Think about the possibility of going for an extra base when the ball is hit through the infield. Listen for the coach's signal to go for it or stay where you are. Swing wide to make the turn easier before going through first base.

*Making contact with the inside of the bag*

- Make contact with the inside corner of the bag as you make your turn. Saving that one step might make all the difference.

- Adjust your running style to the type and conditions of the field. You can go fastest on a dry gravel diamond, for example, while a sandy diamond will slow you down. A wet diamond can also be dangerous as it is harder to stop and turn, so extra care is needed to avoid injuries.

- Don't risk trying for an extra base to get to third or home with none out. If you're tagged out needlessly, you'll deserve all the abuse your team can — and will — dish out.

- Touch all the bases. This sounds obvious and silly, but umpires tell us that they catch at least one missed base per game — usually second or third base. And those are just the ones they actually see.

- When on base, keep the left foot on the ground, touching the side of the bag, not standing on top of it. When the ball is hit, begin

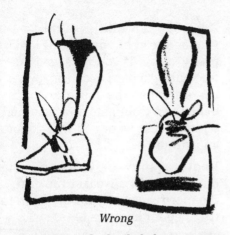

*Wrong*

running with the left foot, crossing it over the right. This take-off will help you build maximum speed.

*Right*

- Know the capabilities of the runner ahead of you. You'll look pretty stupid if you're tagged out for sharing a base because you've overestimated the speed or confidence of a teammate and assumed wrongly that he or she will go for an extra base.

- Know the throwing abilities of the outfielders. The weaker the arm, the more sensible your decision to try to go for an extra base.

- Take advantage of a wet field. It may slow down your running, but it will also slow down the outfielders. A wet ball is hard to catch and throw accurately and quickly, and that's where your advantage lies.

- Watch the third base coach for the signal to go or stay once you leave first base. The coach has the responsibility, so let him take the heat as well. Ignoring the coach costs more runs than it gains.

- With zero or one out, go partway — a third or half the distance — to second base on fly balls hit to shallow or mid-outfield. If the ball is caught, you will have time to get back to first; but if it isn't caught, you will have to hustle to get to second base safely, leaving first open for the hitter.

- With two out, run on any ball including a fly ball. They can only get three out but if the ball is dropped, you're okay.

- Stay on the bag at third on a long fly ball with less than two out. If the ball is caught, the baserunner will be able to make it home without much trouble. If the ball gets past the outfielder or is dropped, the baserunner can still score easily...but missing the run by going out too far and having to come back to third is the worst kind of baserunning sin.

- Time your run past the infielder to be in her or his line of vision when a ground ball is on the way. However, you have to be able to judge the fine line between screening the infielder's view and interfering with the play, for which you will be called out. If

• • • • •     you get hit by the ball while base-
             running you will also be called
             out. (You may also be in pain.)

         •   Don't verbally interfere with the
             infielder trying to catch the ball.
             It's very immature and draws the
             attention of the umpire, who'll
             call you out.

SLIDING  In many leagues, sliding is simply
         not done; in other leagues it's op-
         tional. So be sure of the rules of your
         league before you decide to eat dirt
         for the team. However, the slide is
         one of the most interesting plays, for
         participants and spectators, as it is a
         matter of balancing tactics and
         safety.

             Tactically, it is useful for intimi-
         dating an infielder who is trying to
         concentrate on catching the ball,
         tagging you out or turning the double
         play while your body is coming his
         way in a cloud of dust. Sliding can
         also be dangerous, but may be less so
         than trying to screech to a halt stand-
         ing up after running full tilt to the
         base. Common sense should tell you
         when a slide's worth trying and
         when to play it safe.

These tips will help make best use of a slide, once you've decided one is in order.

- Most slide situations call for the "figure four" slide. Tuck one leg under the other extended leg; extend your arms; slide on your back, not your side.

*"figure four" slide*

- A "hook slide" can keep you from being tagged out on a close play. Aim your body in an arc outside the base so you fall moving away from the tag; hook the bag with your back foot.

*"hook" slide*

- A head-first slide is only for very experienced players, hot dogs and fools. Bear in mind that this slide is the most dangerous — you risk neck, face, shoulder and hand injuries — and then think about it again.

- Be mentally prepared. Decide if you are going to slide or not before the decision has to be made. A last-second notion to slide can risk injury if you can't position your body properly before the slide begins.

- If you decide that sliding is a possibility, wear sliding pads to avoid the scrapes and skin burns that may result.

- Think about sliding early, but begin the actual slide as late as possible. This will tend to throw off the timing of the infielder's throw when attempting a double play. However, be sure to get down quickly. Many infielders will leave it to the runner to get out of the way when they throw the ball.

- Never slide with the intention of hitting the infielder and taking him or her out of the play. It's unsportsmanlike, dangerous and plain stupid.

• • • • •

# 3

# Infield Action

Playing the infield has greater risks and greater potential for glory than playing the outfield. The infielders are expected to move like cats in all directions, catch bullet-like grounders, and throw quickly with perfect accuracy. Those other guys — the ones out there — have only to keep the ball in front of them and get it back to the infield. Nothing to it? Just ask any infielder.

**WHAT EVERY INFIELDER SHOULD KNOW**

Let's face it. The fans that turn out to watch slo-pitch are not legion, but they know their ball. They are also closer to you than they are to the outfielders. This is your opportunity to shine.

- Know how the field surface will affect the movement of the ball, and position yourself accordingly. For example, a loose, sandy field will cause the ball to slow down and to skid rather than bounce. Move in a bit: if you're playing deep in the field, you may not be able to make the throw in time to catch a runner. On the other hand, a hard dirt or gravel surface will cause the ball to bounce straight and hard. Playing deeper will put you in a better fielding position to catch the ball on a bounce.

- Whatever the surface, keep the area around you as clean and smooth as possible. If you get rid of the stray bits of rock and indentations, you are less likely to have a ball take a bounce in a strange, unexpected direction.

- Know your own range in the infield (how far and and how fast you can move). Also, know the range of the other infielders. While two players converging on a ball is better than one, calling for and missing a ball within another player's range is worse.

- You may not be able to get to the ball, but it is important that you're close by to back up the infielder making the play. You probably won't get the runner out but you may pick up a bobbled ball and prevent an attempt to go for an extra base.

- When two players are within range of the ball, the one moving towards the base where the throw will go should take the ball. That player is already moving in the appropriate direction and will be able to field and throw the ball more quickly and accurately than a player who has to back up, stop and then throw.

- An outfielder has priority on a shallow outfield flyball. The infielder should be heading toward the play but should get out of the way once the outfielder yells out that he or she is in position to catch the ball.

- Know the hitters. How strong are they? What part of the field do they tend to hit to? With this information infielders can move towards the area where they expect the ball to be hit. That gives you a better chance to make a play.

- The pitch can give you clues about where the ball might end up when it's hit. For example, a low arc on the pitch tells an infielder to move back. A hit off this ball can come back to the infield faster than one hit off a high arc. Similarly, an outside pitch is likely to be hit towards the opposite field.  • • • • •

- The batter gives you clues as well. Watch the batter's hips to determine his or her stance. An open stance may mean that the batter is trying to pull the ball; a closed stance may indicate he or she is aiming for the opposite field.

- If the batter is known to spray hits all over the park, the outfielders should move in as a challenge. Seeing the infield jammed with defenders, the batter is likely to try to hit over the infield but end up flying out to the outfielders.

- If a batter is known to hit to one side of the field, all the infielders should shift in that direction. (Bear in mind that when there's a left-handed batter the pitcher will have to cover first base.) They should also play farther back in the infield to give them a little more time to react to the hit. In fact, you can go so far as to overman one side of the infield. This ploy works well against a team of ground-ball hitters, if you don't use it too often.

- When possible, move towards a ground ball rather than backing up to get it. The infielder who is moving forward can better handle the bounce, field the ball and throw from a balanced position.

- Try not to blink when a hard-hit ball is coming your way. This sounds very silly, but losing track of the ball even for a split second can make you miss it completely.

- Whenever possible, play on the dirt of the infield rather than the outfield grass. A ball is harder to pick up on grass, bounces are less predictable, and footing is less secure. Leave the grass to the outfielders.

- On an infield hit with men on base, "look" the baserunner back to his base by faking a throw. The good news is that this manoeuvre forces the runner to hesitate, maybe enough to miss an opportunity to gain a base or even a run on an infield hit. The bad news is that infielders sometimes lose their concentration: they are so busy staring down the nearer runner that they do not get off a good throw and lose what should have been a sure out. Very embarrassing.

- Move in a bit closer before the batter swings when you hope to make a double play — but not too close: a ball that you might have caught in your normal fielding position may get through to the outfield. Judge the risk against the speed of the runners.

- Never throw a ball that isn't necessary: chances are you'll throw it badly, hand the opposition an extra base (or a run), and depress your teammates.

- Don't think that you've finished working just because you've got your runner out. Always be ready to make a play to get another runner. All too often infielders are so busy being pleased with themselves for having caught a ball well that they allow a runner to get an extra base.

- Do not obstruct the runners. If you're not involved in making the

• • • • • play or catching the ball, just stay out of their way. Umpires love catching infielders obstructing play.

**INFIELD STANCE**  Infielding is like tightrope walking. You need good balance and the ability to look confident while you work. A large part of the illusion is created by standing in such a way that you look competent, even when you may not be sure what you are doing...or why.

These tips will help you in the infield, if not under the big top.

- Square up your body (everything pointed in the same direction) with your feet about shoulder-width apart. Keep your weight on the balls of your feet, so you can move surely and quickly to either side.

- Get down — with your seat and hips low to the ground — when a ground ball approaches. You have a better chance of blocking the ball in this position than by taking a stylish but not necessarily effective swipe at the ball from an upright position.

*Get down when a ground ball approaches*

- Step toward an incoming ball,
  rather than waiting until the ball
  comes to you. Approach the ball
  with the glove held low and in
  front of the body, which is then in
  position to catch the ball.

• • • • • • When you catch a ball, the leg on your glove side should be forward. This will ensure that your body is in position for throwing the ball.

INFIELD
CATCHING

All slo-pitch players have found balls that seem to have confused their gloves with their heads, arms or shins. As the ball bounces cheerfully off the glove or a piece of your body, you realize this business is harder than it looks.

• Catch the ball in the palm of the glove — not the fingers or the webbing. Make your catch with "soft" hands, moving the hands back as the ball hits the palm. Pretend you're in the raw egg toss at your primary school's sports day.

• Catch the ball with two hands. This not only gives you better control but also greater speed: when the throwing hand is right there as the ball enters the glove, it takes very little time to get the ball out of the glove and make the throw.

- When you are fielding a low, bouncing hit, catch the ball with the fingers of the glove pointing down; then bring the ball up and in towards the body. This softens the impact of the ball and gives you greater control.

*Bring the ball up and in towards the body*

• • • • • • When you're running to catch a ball in foul territory, move quickly to the fence. Then move back from the fence to make the actual catch. You'll be in a better position to catch the ball without unexpected interference from an inanimate object.

INFIELD THROWING Infielders can find a time and place for every throw going: overhand, sidearm, and underhand. It depends on the game situation and the timing of the play. It also depends on what feels comfortable for the infielder doing the throwing, as well as his or her age and the strength of the throwing arm in question. These tips will help you throw more accurately and effectively.

• Grip the ball with two fingers and the thumb. The fingers should be across the seams; the thumb should be under the ball. Grasping the ball this way gives you better control, accuracy and speed than gripping it with three or four fingers plus thumb.

*Grip the ball with two fingers and the thumb*

- Make sure the pivot foot (the one you end up on) is planted firmly and follow through with the throw. As your body moves through the throw, the shoulder of your throwing arm should point in the direction you are aiming the ball. With luck the ball will end up moving in that direction as well.

*Make sure the pivot foot is planted firmly*

- As a general rule, aim a long
  throw at the chest of the player
  who will be catching the ball.
  This is a good compromise position: if your throw is a little high
  or a bit low, the player should be
  able to adjust his or her stance to
  catch it. However, you should
  also be aware of the height at
  which teammates prefer to catch a
  ball. For example, some players

tend not be very effective at catching low balls. (This is a particular hazard when the player is wearing bifocals, and the ball goes from the size of a pea to that of a grapefruit in nanoseconds!)

- A full overhand throw will give you the most speed and greatest accuracy. It's also easiest on the arm muscles. This throw is particularly important for the third baseman and shortstops, who tend to make the long throws to first base.

- Everyone's sidearm throw moves somewhat differently, so make sure you adjust your aim to accommodate the amount of spin you get on the throw. (This spin tends to cause the ball to tail away from the target.)

- When you flip a little underhand ball to an infielder (usually when forcing out a runner or starting the double play), aim at the catching player's chest. This makes your toss easier to control and easier to catch.

There's more to communication than "I got it, I got it, I got it" as you go chasing after the ball, oblivious to the rest of the world. Communication is essential to a team's ability to make the right play at the right time. When that time comes, you don't have the luxury of deciding who will call for the ball and who will throw to whom. This has to be worked out before play starts. Effective communication can be worked out logically and simply, and can have the effect of avoiding the botched play and the disappointed shrugs of teammates.

- Make sure each player knows the essentials of the situation: how many out, the score in the game, and the potential danger of this particular at-bat.

- Before the pitch is thrown, make sure all the players know what plays are possible, where they are going to throw the ball, etc.

- Choose the play that is the most likely to succeed. Why risk an easily botched double-play attempt or the spectacular but dodgy long throw when there's a • • • • • sure out right there for the taking.

- However, don't take for granted that everyone knows which play is the obvious choice. Keep everyone informed and "in the game."

- Yell for the ball only when you can guarantee your teammates you'll get the batter out.

- When the ball is coming in from the outfielder, the catching infielder (cut-off man) should be told whether and where he or she should throw the ball. The second baseman and shortstop usually work in tandem on this information: one does the catching, the other yells over the information.

- When you call other infielders off a pop fly, yell LOUDLY, making sure they hear you. Otherwise, one of two things will happen: you will collide with another infielder, which can be very, very painful; or, you will both pull up and wait for the other to catch the ball. In either case the ball will drop to the turf and you will,

• • • • • rightly, feel foolish and perhaps bruised.

• Don't give other infielders a hard time after they've botched a play. Be supportive in the name of team spirit and the hope that they will be equally forgiving when the error is yours.

TAGGING Tagging a runner takes nerve, aggressiveness and concentration. You have to have nerve not simply to bail out of the way when 230 lbs of beef is bearing down on the base you are protecting. A certain amount of aggressiveness is needed to make the play with enough authority that the umpire can see that it has been made. And you have to be able to concentrate on the movement of the ball and ignore the dust, noise and snorting of the aforementioned lout headed your way.

Here are a few tips to get your runner and get out alive

• While you wait for the throw, keep your feet on either side of the bag. Then you will be aware of the exact position of the bag throughout whatever strange or exciting play develops.

• • • • •

*Keep your feet on either side of the bag*

- Keep your body low, over or just in front of the bag. This might intimidate the approaching runner and blocks easy access to the bag.

- When running to tag a runner between first and second base on a double play attempt, keep your bare hand on the ball while it is in

57

the glove. Tag the runner with the back of the glove so your bare hand is in position to bring the ball out quickly and make the play to first that will complete the double play.

*Keep your bare hand on the ball*

- When you want to tag a sliding baserunner, keep the glove so that it is in front of the base and touching the ground. With the ball safely in the glove, supported by the bag, the runner will slide into the outside of the glove and will have little chance of dislodging the ball. This type of tag is much more reliable than sweeping or reaching with the gloved ball toward the runner.

*Reliable tagging*

- When making a tag at third base, keep the feet widely placed on either side of the bag. This position will lessen the danger of foot injuries and allows you to lean over the bag with both hands outstretched to make the catch and the tag on the incoming runner.
- Whenever possible, keep two hands on the ball while tagging a runner.

- Tag a sliding runner low on the body. Umpires often declare baserunners safe if they are tagged high up during a slide. They figure that the feet must have made it to the bag before the tag touched the upper body.

- Don't fake a tag on a runner when you don't have the ball. This can be dangerous and, depending on the rules of your slo-pitch league, might get you ejected from the game.

**DEFENSIVE PLAYS**

There are a couple of moments in slo-pitch when you are poised on the brink of either making a brilliant play or bringing on disaster. You usually can't anticipate these moments, and they happen so fast you can often miss them entirely, whether you are a player or spectator. Two playing situations that produce such moments are the rundown play and the infield fly. In both cases, presence of mind is the deciding factor. With it, you can be a hero or at least an asset to the team. Without it, you have no choice but to throw yourself on the mercy of your teammates.

Oh the joy of the rundown — when the runner gets caught between the bases and the infielders toss the ball back and forth until they tag the poor sod out. Few things in slo-pitch are more satisfying. Unless you're the runner.

First, here are a few general tips for the infielders; then we'll describe two typical rundown situations.

- Throw the ball as few times as possible. The more you toss the ball, the more likely you are to mess up. One or two throws should be enough. More and you'll be courting disaster.

- If the runner is going to get to a base safely, make sure the one he or she started from is the best chance.

- If you're not involved in the play, back up the players who are involved. Be ready to step in, for example if a player is out of position after he or she throws the ball.

*Back up the players*

- If you are involved in the play run right at the baserunner to force him or her to commit to one direction or the other. This doesn't mean you have to act like Attila the Hun: you can remain a good sport while making a decisive play.

Now, here's a typical situation involving second and third base:

(a) The third baseman runs towards the baserunner, throws the ball to the second baseman, and gets out of the way; then

(b) the second baseman runs towards third, throws to the short-stop, who has stepped in to cover for the third baseman, and gets out of the way; then

(c) the pitcher comes in to cover for the second baseman, ready to take the throw if needed.

(d) the key here is to cover and then peel off after making the play.

Here's a typical play involving third base and home plate. (Assume the ball has been hit to the infield, that there is no force play at the plate and only one out.) The runner on third is trying to score.

(a) The catcher takes the throw and runs toward the baserunner.

If the third baseman is in a position to make the tag:

(b) the catcher throws her or him the ball; then

(c) the third baseman follows the runner toward the plate and makes the tag, while staring down the hitter to try to keep her or him from trying to get to second, rather than staying at first.

If the third baseman is NOT in a position to make the tag:
(b) the third baseman throws the ball to the pitcher, who is covering home plate for the catcher; then
(c) the shortstop covers third base, just in case, while the first and second basemen cover their bases, ready for a play on the batter.

INFIELD FLY     We all know the infield fly rule, right? Of course we do: If there are fewer than two outs, and if first and second bases are occupied (third can be occupied or not), and if a hitter pops up a fly to the infield, then the hitter is automatically declared out and the runners can try to advance at their own risk.

Now, here is a play that is legal, but considered mean-spirited except in very competitive situations. In

friendly play it will earn you cat-
calls rather than curtain calls. Now
that you've been warned, here goes:

Rather than just catching the fly
ball to get it in play, let it hit the
ground before you catch it. An
unthinking runner may jump and
attempt to advance, as we said, at
his own risk. It may just turn into an
easy out, if your missing the ball act
has fooled him.

• • • • •

# 4 *Infield Positions*

• • • **PITCHER**

Due to the hitability of the highly arced pitch that defines the game, slo-pitch pitchers do not usually control a game the way pitchers can in fast pitch or baseball. In fact, in many slo-pitch leagues, all sorts of players, strong and weak, end up pitching at one time or another. Precisely because slo-pitch is much less likely to be dominated by its pitching, the slo-pitch pitcher's success is more easily influenced by the play of his or her teammates: they can save you or ruin you. However, there are a couple of ways in which pitchers can lose a game all by themselves: walking the batters and throwing pitches that are easy to hit. No team, however brilliant on the defence can save you from these basic errors. These tips, on the other hand, might help you save yourself

• Know the batters, as most of them are creatures of habit. Know the ones who swing at the first ball no matter what and the ones who can only hit deep into the outfield. Give the batter every pitch but the one you know he or she likes to hit. Some balls will trick certain batters every time: know your victim!

- Make sure the rest of your team is in position in the infield and outfield before you start your pitch. Take a second or two to survey the field and make sure all your stalwarts are where they should be. Then give all your attention to the batter.

- Concentrate on the weak hitters. Good hitters will hit anyway, so concentrate on neutralizing the weak ones and keep the team from getting on a roll.

- Don't let your pitches get too flat. The ones arced at eleven feet are tougher to hit than the relatively flat six footers. Your fielders will thank you for keeping the ball "up".

- Keep them guessing as to which of your many possible pitches you are going to throw. Throw some inside, some outside, some extra high, and the occasional one short. As long as you are around

• • • • •  the strike zone, you'll keep the
batters wondering what's coming
next.

• Vary the timing of your pitches to
keep the batters off guard. You
may be able to rush nervous
batters, while taking time to make
the most of every pitch to better
batters.

• After the pitch is thrown, a good
pitcher becomes a fielder. Many
hits come back through the centre.
It pays to be ready for them.

• Move backwards after pitching
the ball. This can confuse the
batter as it adds background
movement while the batter is
trying to block out all motion but
that of the ball. By moving back
you also put yourself into position
to cover more of the infield;
however, there's a price. It's
harder to field a ball when moving backwards than to catch it
standing still or moving toward it.

• If the ball is hit back to you, throw
over strongly to the infielder,
rather than trying to lob the ball.

You are more likely to make a good throw when you release the ball normally. Anything "unnatural", such as a lob or a flip, takes thinking and deprives you of your practised, instinctive throw.

- Even when an umpire declares a pitch illegal, the batter has the option of hitting it. For example, many hitters will go for an illegal flat pitch (under six foot arc). Be prepared to field no matter what kind of garbage you've pitched.

  All players on the field must know the positions they should cover, and which player they should be backing up on each play. The pitchers' covering assignments are the most complicated.

- Get behind the third baseman to cover all throws to that bag, especially ones coming in from the outfield.

- There are two occasions when you should be covering second base. The main one is when the infield (and outfield) is playing

• • • • • well back because a powerful
hitter is up. The other occasion is
when a throw is coming in from
left or centre. Your being there
will prevent an inaccurate throw
from getting loose and allowing
the runners extra bases.

- Be the cutoff man on throws from
centre field to home. Your job is
to prevent runners from advanc-
ing past first and second. However, listen for the catcher to yell,
"let it go" on throws that can get
all the way to the plate in time to
make a play at home.

- Keep your eyes open for runners
who miss touching a base. It's
quite common for at least one
base to be missed per game. A
timely appeal to the umpire and
the subsequent calling out of the
runner can make the difference in
a close game.

CATCHER   In baseball, catchers are usually the
pitchers' brains and often the infielders' eyes. In slo-pitch, however,
catchers are often inexperienced
players hidden behind the plate

where they can't do too much damage. However, catchers can be the game strategists and commanders of the infield. As they have the same view of the field as batters do, good catchers can set the defence to best advantage. Here are a few ideas on how to play the catcher's position to its full potential.

*Give the pitcher a good clear target*

- Place your glove so that you give the pitcher a good clear target to throw at.

- Wear a trapper rather than the standard glove, unless it's against your league's rules (which it usually isn't). A trapper is larger than the normal glove often worn by first basemen and gives you a larger catching area and a surer grip on the ball when you're tagging a runner.

- Keep the rest of the team involved: let them know the count against the batter and the number of outs.

- Know the batters' hitting habits, so you can shift the fielders and effectively anticipate the direction of the hit ball.

- Keep the batters off guard with some friendly chatter. Asking about the family, commenting on the great-looking pitch that's coming in, etc. can unnerve them without being considered unethical. Save the hard-core stuff for the final game of a tournament against small guys who won't fight back.

- Be both friendly and humble in your conversations with the umpire. He or she may pay no attention, but then he or she just might give you the benefit of a doubt when you need it most.

- Don't jump up too quickly when catching a pitched ball. You may block the umpire's vision and he or she will feel obliged to call it a ball, even if it was right over the centre of the plate.

- Don't get overzealous: reaching forward too quickly for a pitched ball may earn you a bat on the hand or the back of the head. Painful.

- Pop fouls generally move to the open side, i.e., away from the batter.

- When going for a pop fly, turn toward the ball, take off the mask and locate the ball. Then — and only then — throw the mask well out of the way so you won't trip over it going for the catch.

- Blocking the plate may be heroic, but it can also be physically dangerous, for both catcher and baserunner. Simply blocking the plate, and not making a tag play, is obstruction. The umpire will call the runner safe at home in spite of your bulk being in the way. However, if there is a play on at the plate, move a few feet toward third base to tag the runner if you can. This is legal, effective, and you'll be able to get up to go to work the next morning.

- Always be ready to field the "full-swing bunt" barehanded. Bunts are illegal, of course, but those near misses that drop five feet in front of the plate need fast reactions and a quick throw to first. There's no time to use your glove.

- When a ball is hit to the infield, cover behind the first baseman provided there are no runners on base. If there are runners, stay at home in case a play comes there.

- When a throw is coming into third base, you may have to back up the third baseman. Before you

head that way, however, make
sure the first baseman is coming
in to cover home plate and the
pitcher isn't already covering
third. Otherwise, stay where you
are.

Players at this position should have
absolutely solid catching skills: they
need to be able to nab the ball when
it's high, low and to either side.
They also have to field bouncers and
wild throws from both infield and
outfield. In short, they have to make
everyone look good except the batter. In order to play first base effectively and avoid missing the ball in
tough situations, try these tips

FIRST BASE

- Never just be a spectator in the
  game: always assume you will be
  part of the action on the play.
  (Truth is, of course, that often as
  not there's lots of time off, time
  enough to get complacent and
  take too long to react to the play.)

- Move quickly to the base when
  the ball has been hit. Straddle the
  bag. Once you see which way the
  ball is coming in, you can touch

• • • • • the bag with whichever foot allows you to stretch towards the ball.

• However, don't stretch too early. It's easy to miss a ball if you are already in a stretch position and the ball curves away from exactly where you expected it to be.

• Catch the ball even if you have to leave the bag to do it. Staying on the bag at all costs simply means the ball — and the runner — will get away from you.

• When there is a righthanded batter, position yourself about one third of the way to second parallel to the bag.

• When there is a lefthanded batter, position yourself about five feet behind the bag and close enough to the line to be able to catch a ball that's hit just barely in fair territory.

• Be prepared to act as a cut-off man on a ball thrown down the line from right-field to home plate. Position yourself in a straight line between the fielder and the catcher when your catching the ball might hold a runner on base or put out a baserunner. Listen for the catcher to call you off the ball so it will go through to homeplate.

- If there is not a runner on first, cover home plate when the catcher has gone to cover third base.

## SECOND BASE

The second baseman works in tandem with the shortstop to create infield double plays. The position takes intense concentration and quick reaction time, especially when a baserunner is bearing down on you like a tractor trailer on glare ice. Here are some tips to help you survive

- Know the batters. Know where they are likely to hit the ball before it is pitched. Then let the shortstop know whether to cover second base for you if you figure you can field the ball.
- Stretch for the ball like a first baseman in order to force out a runner at second.

- Take most of the fly balls behind first base. Obviously it is easier for the second baseman to run back at an angle than for the first baseman to run straight backwards.

- Know your range and that of the first baseman, so you can effectively field balls that go between first and second. When fielding a ground ball, the second baseman should play deeper than the first baseman. In that position you can make the play if it is hit too far for the first baseman or provide backup in case the ball gets away from him or her.

- Ignore the baserunner coming into second when you are turning towards first to attempt a double play. You must concentrate only on the first baseman. Let incoming runners risk a mouthful of softball (neither soft nor tasty) if they don't get out of your way.

- Be prepared to relay or cut off the ball from the outfielder when it has been hit to right or right-centre field. Position yourself between the outfielder and the

base where the play should be
made.

They don't call this the "hot corner"
for nothing: balls rocket in with
little time for the third baseman to
react. You have to be able to catch
the ball on one hop and throw it
accurately all the way to first base —
no mean task.

Here are some tips to make third
base easier to play

- When a righthanded batter is up,
  position yourself about five to ten
  feet behind the third base bag.
  You should also be close enough
  to the line to be able to catch a
  ball that is hit just barely fair.

- When a lefthanded batter is up,
  position yourself on a line with
  the second and third base bags,
  about a third of the way toward
  second base. Left-handed third
  basemen can often safely manage
  a position a few steps closer to
  second due to their gloves being
  on the right side.

- Keep your glove in position ready
  to catch: in front of your body
  about knee level. With so little

• • • • • time to react to the ball, anything that gains you a split second is worthwhile.

• Let the shortstop catch most of the flyballs hit directly behind third base. It is easier for him or her to move backwards at an angle than for you to move straight backwards to make a catch.

• Know your range as well as that of the shortstop, so the two of you can work out a strategy for fielding balls that come between your positions. (More balls are hit between third and short than right down the line to third.)

• Be prepared to relay or cut off balls from left field to the plate. Listen for the catcher for instructions to let the ball go directly to home without your help.

• Position your feet so they widely straddle the bag when you are tagging out a runner. This position will prevent injuries from an incoming slide and allows you to lean out over the bag toward the ball and runner to make the tag.

Shortstops are usually the best all-round athletes on the team. They have to have the quickest reaction time, the greatest range, excellent catching skills and strong throwing arms. Often as not the shortstop turns out to be the player who is youngest, best-looking, fittest, and most likely to have a cheering section in the stands. Usually, none of this surprises them.

If you already have the looks, stamina, and know you're the centre of the universe, here are a few tips to bring your playing up to your level of confidence.

- Position yourself about one third to half way from second to third base, well behind the bases to give you as much time as possible to get the ball. (Throwing hard and fast from this position to first base is where the need for a strong throwing arm comes in.)

- When a double play may be possible, work out your strategy with the second baseman before each play as to who will cover the base and make the throw to first.

- Most of the fly balls hit directly behind third base should be your responsibility rather than that of the third baseman. It is easier for you to angle over to catch them than for the third baseman to run straight backwards.

- When a ball is hit to left or left-centre field, be prepared to cut off or relay the ball from the fielder to the base where the throw should go.

- When two outfielders are both going for the ball and calling off the other, call the name of the fielder most likely to make the catch. This will warn the other player to back off and may well avert a dangerous collision.

- As the best athlete on the team, the shortstop should also be a team leader. Don't get down on yourself or other players when things are not going well. Be encouraging and lead by example.

# Outfield Action and Positions

Slo-pitch outfielders are either
heroes or bums. Only by keeping
their heads as alert as their gloves
and throwing arms do they avoid
catching that easy fly ball on a
bounce or miss it entirely. Here are
some tips on making a difference in
the field:

- Get to know the field: how the
  ball rebounds from fences,
  screens and scoreboards; how
  wide the warning track is; and
  what (if anything) the back fence
  or wall is made of — in case you
  bounce off it.

- Note the weather and condition of
  the playing surface. For example,
  a wet field is slow: ground balls
  slow down quickly; line drives
  tend to skid rather than bounce,
  and so on. On wet days footing
  can be treacherous, making
  catches tricky and throws sloppy.

- Know the batters. They tend to be
  predictable after a while, so you
  should be able to judge where to
  position yourself in the field to be
  waiting for the hit. Gutsy fielders
  can play shallow but risk looking

• • • • •   like fools if the ball sails over
their heads and they have to chase
it like a dog after a stick. Overly
timid fielders play so deep they
might as well hop the fence into
the stands for all the difference
they make to the game. So remember, position yourself for the
current batter and playing situation. Keep alert.

• Keep an eye on the speed of the
baserunners. Knowing who is
very quick and who lumbers will
help you decide which base has
the best chance of a play on any
hit.

• Be aware of the score, the count
on the batter, how many are out
and whether tying or winning
runs are on base. All of these will
have an impact on how you play
the ball and where you should
throw it.

• Know the speed of your infielders. If one is particularly slow,
you will want to head in early
towards a shallow fly ball.

• Always assume the infield is
going to miss a catch: back up the
play, just in case you're needed.

Be in a position to field any ball that may come through the infield. There will be many of them!

- Assess your infielders' weaknesses. Knowing how well they can move to left and right will help you anticipate which balls will squirt through them to the outfield.

- Be aware of the other outfielders' strengths and weaknesses so your play can complement and compensate for theirs. Always move to back up the play of the adjacent outfielder in case the ball gets past him or her.

- Play aggressively. Not only is running for all you're worth and making diving catches a good example to the rest of the team, but you will successfully field more of the short plays that get the runners out. You will also get your uniform dirty, which confirms that you made it off the bench. (The downside is that you will allow some doubles and triples; but you'll have a better record of outs over the long haul.)

**OUTFIELD CATCHING**

This sounds self-explanatory. After all, what else do outfielders do? However, there's more to catching than simply putting out the old mitt. Here are a few ways of making outfield plays look routine. (Making routine plays look spectacular is your problem!)

- Catch the ball with "soft hands". Moving the hands back as the ball enters the glove discourages the ball from bouncing out again.

- Allow the ball to be caught by the outfielder who is in the best position to catch it and get it quickly back to the infield. (Usually this means the fielder who is moving forward toward the ball.) Selfish outfielders often give in to uncontrollable urges to be the hero: diving for a ball that another outfielder could catch more easily. The result could be an extra base needlessly given.

- Call an infielder off a fly ball if you have a better chance of making the catch. (Outfielders have priority over infielders in this case.)

- When calling for a fly ball, yell
  loudly and wave your mates off
  with both arms: make it obvious
  that you want to make the catch
  so the other players can bail out
  before you run full tilt into them.

*Wave your mates off*

- When fielding a ground ball,
  make sure you keep the ball in
  front of your body. Go down on
  one knee, keeping the body
  squared front to block the incoming ball. If you miss the catch,
  chances are the ball will hit your
  body (rather than get past you).
  You can then pick the ball up and
  keep the runner from gaining an
  extra base.

*Fielding a ground ball*

- Run back to the fence on a deep
  fly ball. Then turn and run forward toward the place just behind
  the spot where the ball is expected to fall. (You will then be
  prepared to step forward into the
  catch and throwing position in
  one smooth motion.) It is always
  better to catch a ball while moving forwards. Attempting a catch
  while moving backwards is risky:

not only might you injure yourself but the ball may drop when you hit the fence.

• Inexperienced outfielders often run back for the ball with one arm in the air ready for the catch. This not only looks silly (and betrays your inexperience) but slows your running. Just run like hell and worry about catching the ball when you're closer to it.

• When there is a runner on third base and less than two runners out, decide whether trying to catch a fly ball in foul territory is worth the risk. (The runner may tag and then try to get home after the ball is caught.) The game situation may make the gamble of letting the ball drop worthwhile.

## OUTFIELD THROWING

It's one thing to catch the ball, and quite another to know what to do with it once it is safely in your glove. The key is to know what play you should make before you catch the ball. Here's how to make the right move every time:

• • • • • • Remember who the cut-off man is in every possible situation, and know how to hit him or her when the ball comes through the infield. There's nothing more humiliating than hearing someone yell, "C'mon guys let's throw to the cut-off man!" Especially when you know it's *you* that they're really yelling at.

• It's most often quicker to throw it to the cut-off player and for that player to relay it to the plate than to make one long throw to home.

• Before you catch the ball, know where you'll throw it. Once you do catch the ball, throw it immediately. Don't hang on to the ball as if you've finished your job.

• Never throw behind the baserunner. It often means the runner can easily make the next base. He or she wouldn't try for it, or you may have a play if you had thrown the ball ahead of him or her.

LEFT FIELDER    Players at this position are usually the second strongest outfielder. Being left-handed makes it easier to catch balls in foul territory without having to run past the ball or catch the ball back-handed. (Having a thick skin is also an advantage: how far away can a left fielder be from vociferous fans?)

## RIGHT FIELDER

Most hitters are right-handed and therefore likely to hit to left or centre-left field, so it is in these positions that you need the strongest fielders. So it seems inevitable that the right field is often a place to hide a weak player. However, the right fielder can help his or her own cause if he or she catches left handed (and can therefore better cover down the line) and has a strong arm to make those long throws to third base. (Skin thicker than that required of a left fielder is also an advantage. The fans will assume you're in right field because there's nowhere else to put you, aside from catcher of course.)

## CENTRE FIELD

Depending on the hitting abilities of the teams you play, centre field can be played in one of two ways. Against long ball hitting teams, two

• • • • • centre fielders playing deep are used. Against "singles" hitting teams, a rover can be very effective.

**ROVER**    Sometimes a rover plays in conjunction with the centre fielder, usually playing shallow in the gaps behind the shortstop or second baseman. As such, the rover is most effective against teams that hit for singles all over the park rather than against sluggers aiming for the home run over the fence.

On a hard hit ball through the infield, the rover can often throw the runner out at first, or make a force play at second, third or even home.

Rather than keep him or her as the other centre fielder, often teams will quickly move in a rover just before the play to the surprise and demise of the spray hitting batter.

**CENTRE FIELDER**    When there is no rover, the left-centre fielder is generally the strongest outfielder. He or she and the right-centre fielder should be the best runners in the outfield, as they have the largest territory to cover. They have priority on balls hit

anywhere near their territory; the
left and right fielders should act as
backup on these plays.

    The centre fielders should be the
"quarterbacks" of the outfield, warning the other fielders about field
conditions, telling them where the
batters are likely to hit, and posi-
tioning the field accordingly. They
should also coach the other fielders
about balls coming their way.
(Centre fielders have the best angle
on the trajectory of the hit ball.)

# 6 *Coaching*

Coaching is a people management job as well as task management one. Leadership is essential, particularly leading by example. Learn, and live by, the ethics of the game and your league.

Players, like most employees, don't like surprises. Tell your players your personal objectives for the team. Listen to their input. Make sure you have a match between their objectives and yours. Tell them what your strategy will be for batting orders, sit-out plans, and most of all, avoid publicly criticizing your players. If you have a comment on a bonehead play, make it individually, after the play or after the game. Ensure that you and your team refrain from yelling out to a player who has just done something he or she had absolutely no intention of doing...like botching a play.

Everyone wants to do well and contribute to the team. Get the most out of them...encourage them to play to the best of their ability, knowing what their ability realistically is.

In slo-pitch, as in most organized amateur sports, there are those who are naturally gifted at coaching. There are also those who reluctantly volunteer for the job because no one else wants to do it. Some teams, short even of volunteers, simply give coaching duties to the players sitting out any given inning.

We think these tips will be useful for coaches of every level of expertise:

## COACHING THE BASES

The cardinal rule for choosing base coaches is this: make sure that they are knowledgeable ballplayers. These are no positions for the player who knows little about strategy and game situations. So often, a player will "take first" or "take third" just to get a better view of the game, without any thought of how he or she can help the team by helping the runners.

Base coaches can be the most important offensive tools on the field, with their ability to manufacture runs through smart coaching techniques. They can also save overzeal-

• • • • • ous runners from the embarassment of running into an easy out.

There is a downside, however, to base coaching. Not every decision results in that extra base being made. Teams should appreciate that, if the coach makes a mistake, he or she lives with it. It's not the end of the world...although it might mean the end of the game. The pressure does come with the job, so let them get on with it...and follow their instructions whether you think you can make that extra base or not.

FIRST BASE
COACH

- Tell the runner coming to first base whether to stop, round the base and wait, or go on to second base. Don't be subtle: yell and wave your arms so your message is clear.

- Tell the runner on first the number of outs and the count on the batter. Remind him or her of all the situations that might arise on the next play.

- When the ball is hit, you are the eyes of the runner on first. Tell the runner what to do: tag up, go half way or all the way to second.

- Stand so that you are clearly visible to the runner coming toward you from the plate. Be even with or slightly back from the bag and as close to the first base line as the coach's box allows.

- Encourage the approaching runner to hustle when the play looks close. You can see what's going on around the runner, who may be concentrating only on the bag.

## THIRD BASE COACH

The job of coaching third base should be given to your most knowledgeable player. (This is no place for the nerd who can't play but wants to feel part of the team.) However, you need only one third-base coach: if your team occupies the dug-out on the third-base line, tell the players not to yell instructions to the baserunner. It will confuse the runner and lose potential runs.

- Always be ready to make a quick decision: be aware of the game

- situation and plays that might arise at all times.

- Ignore the yahoos in the crowd (or on the bench): stick to your decisions. Once made, follow your decisions through to avoid potential injury to the baserunner or lost runs.

- Position yourself clearly in the baserunner's line of vision. Be right behind the bag as the runner comes straight in to third. Stand ten or fifteen feet along the base line towards home for the runner who's looking for instructions to stay on third or go for home. Let the baserunner know early what you've decided. A late decision and a screaming stop might injure your player.

- Watch how the outfielders handle the ball. If the outfielder catches the ball on the run toward the infield, your runner has less time and you might want to hold him or her on base. If the outfielder is backpedalling or running to either side, he will need a bit more time to stop and set up his throw. You might then tell your runner to go for the extra base.

- Make your verbal instructions clear. Don't use words that can be confused when signalling the runner. ("Whoa," "no," and "go" are obviously useless in this situation!) You can reinforce your verbal instructions with body signals:

STOP:

*Arms out front*

• • • • •  SLIDE:

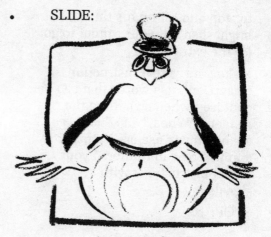

*Arms out, palms down*

EASE IN:

*Arms up high*

GO:                                              • • • • •

*Windmilling arms*

- Instruct the on-deck batter to
  become a coach, giving the signal
  to ease-in or slide to the runner
  coming toward home plate.

If there was a prize for the most          **ESTABLISHING**
controversial coaching decision, a         **THE BATTING**
unanimous vote would go to the             **ORDER**
batting order. Your place in the
order often is seen to reflect your
character, talents, and any other
aspect of your person that you are
sensitive about. Finding yourself

batting fifteenth is like being picked last in the draft.

What you need is a bit of perspective. We're all grown-ups, right? Well, we'll rephrase that: we all know the team is more important than the individual players, right? Be mature about it: think about the coach's problems. There are as many schools of thought on the batting order as there are coaches. How do you choose one that works? Here are a few approaches:

- **The Safe Method:**

  Look at your most recent on-base statistics and line up your players in descending order.

  This may make the coach look indecisive to some players. However, many coaches argue that it's worth it for the incentive it provides to the players to play well enough to move up in the order.

  One argument in favour of putting the sure hitters (and fastest baserunners) at the top of the order and letting the rest of the line-up take care of itself is that you increase your chances of getting an early lead, thus building morale and intimidating the other team.

- ## The Strong/Weak Method

Structure your order with your strongest hitter first, a weak player second, your second strongest hitter third, a weak player fourth, etc. This ensures that there is always a reasonably good player coming to the plate in each inning. Unfortunately, in many house leagues, it means there's a "rally killer" on his way to the plate soon after.

This is not a very popular method: most coaches consider it a waste of good hitters who, if clumped together could get on base and around to score.

- ## The Scientific Method:

This is generally thought to be the most reasonable and reliable. Start your lineup with a few players who are "sure" to get on base. Follow up with a power hitter to move them home. Then

• • • • •   mix up your remaining weak and strong hitters, making sure not to leave a clump of weak hitters together at the bottom of the order.

SIT-OUTS   In most slo-pitch leagues, teams have more than the standard roster of ten players. As many as fifteen players may alternate in and out of the game. In most house leagues a rule ensures that all players get roughly equal playing time. (Some mixed leagues also insist that there be a certain number of women on the field in every inning, so the women may get more playing time than the men, if your team is un-evenly divided.) Constructing a roster to accommodate all these rules takes time and concentration. There are a couple of ways to do this:

• Number each player. Say you have twelve players out for a game: sit out numbers one and two in the first inning, three and four in the second, etc. (Obvi-ously, you will sit out more or fewer players depending on the total number of players on your team.)

- Assign two or three players to each position. Sit out as many as you need to at any time, in rotation.

- Have the better players sit out the middle innings of the game: save them for the crucial early and late innings.

- Figure out what specific skills you will need in each inning. Then figure out which players you can do without, on an inning-by-inning basis.

Whatever method you choose, draw up a chart of who will play what position when, and post it before game time. Players will then have time to get used to what is going to happen and will be able to mentally prepare for what will be asked of them. This is an effective way of maximizing players' performance and morale.

Suffice it to say that "if you want to play to win you have to practise to win." Practice is essential if you

**Practices**

• • • • • want to get the most out of your
team.

- Pitching machines are quite popular and a lot of people swear by
  them. One observation is that the
  arc pitched by some pitching
  machines is too low for slo-pitch.
  Look for ones that give the charac-
  teristic eleven or twelve foot high
  trajectory.

- A batting tee — like the kind
  young kids use — is very benefi-
  cial for practising swings, placing
  the ball, and building consistency.
  It's also good for mental prepara-
  tion. It allows a player to practise
  alone: all you need is a bag of
  balls.

# Conditioning and Stretching

No, we are not going to get all preachy. We know you don't have the lithe, fit body you pretend you used to have. We don't either. Fitness à la Fonda or Schwarzenegger? To hell with it — it's a lost cause.

Be that as it may, basic, non-neurotic conditioning does have its uses: to avoid illness, maintain a cheerful sense of general well-being, and prevent catastrophic degeneration of the body. (Your mind is your own problem.) It also qualifies you to be intolerably self-righteous about the true slobs of this world.

If you can travel a mile on a fairly flat surface in twelve minutes or less, you can begin a fairly respectable training program, provided your doctor says it's OK. (If you don't qualify, start out with something easy, like watching sports on TV.)

If you feel any pain, shortness of breath or general discomfort after conditioning or playing, confess to your doctor and abide by his or her professional advice.

Stretching is the world's perfect pre-activity activity. It's easy and doesn't require expensive equip-

• • • • • ment, health-club membership, or Spandex. There is no hidden agenda. All it does is:
(a) prepare your body for movement, which is essential for people like us who loaf around all day; and
(b) keep your body from cramping after the game.

In your newly flexible body you will also be less likely to incur stupid injuries, especially early in the slo-pitch season. Moreover, you can think about the game instead of about what you're going to feel like next morning.

We take back that bit about there being no hidden agenda. Stretching is an insidious activity. After a while you get to like it. You may even do it when you don't have to. (There have even been cases of players dropping the ball just to prove they can bend down and pick it up without straining their hamstrings.)

Also, a pre-game stretch engenders respect and awe from players and fans. Everyone will be convinced you know what you're doing, at least until the game begins. Such unquestioning adulation is usually experienced only by rock stars, TV evangelists and plumbers who work weekends.

Our slo-pitch stretching routine has been designed by Coleene Wilson, practising Physio/Occupational Therapist and slo-pitch player. It should be done one half hour before play begins and immediately after the game to reduce the risk of injury during the season. It can also be done in the off-season to lessen the initial shock of opening day.

The routine is easy to remember. Stand for eight exercises, sit for two, and lie down for two. (Ah! Feel's better already.) Then finish with a lunge and a trot.

All these stretches should be done slowly and smoothly. Don't bounce the body into the stretching position: you may injure your muscles.

If the routine seems too rigorous for you, sneak up on it. Do a few of each type of stretch and you will probably find you can do more and more as the season progresses.

So here we go:

**STRETCH No. 1**
PURPOSE: To stretch the calf muscles.
POSITION: Face a wall. Place the toes
of the right foot against the wall, an
inch or two off the ground, keeping
the heel on the ground. Keep the knee
and hip straight.
ACTION: Lean into the wall until you
feel the calf muscle stretch. Hold that
position for a count of ten. Repeat
nine times. Repeat stretch sequence
with your left foot against the wall.

**STRETCH No. 2**
PURPOSE: To stretch upper thigh
and groin muscles.
POSITION: Stand on left foot.
ACTION: Bring right foot up toward
right buttock, bending the right knee
while keeping the right hip straight.
Hold for a count of ten. Repeat nine
times. Repeat stretch sequence with
left foot.

**STRETCH No. 3**

PURPOSE: To stretch muscles in the back of the thigh.

POSITION: Stand with feet shoulder-width apart. Place right foot ahead of left foot.

ACTION: Bend forward at the waist, reaching down to touch right toe or the ground in front of it, if you can. Hold position for a count of ten. Repeat nine times. Repeat stretch sequence with left foot forward.

**STRETCH No. 4**
PURPOSE: To stretch the lower back muscles.
POSITION: Stand with legs slightly apart.
ACTION: Pull up right knee to chest. Hold for a count of ten. Repeat nine times. Repeat stretch sequence holding left knee.

**STRETCH No. 5**
PURPOSE: To stretch the muscles of the trunk.
POSITION: Stand with hands on hips. Keep hips and lower body facing forward.
ACTION: Turn upper body to the right. Hold position for a count of ten. Repeat nine times slowly and smoothly. Repeat stretch sequence, turning to the left.

**STRETCH No. 6**
PURPOSE: To stretch the triceps
muscles.
POSITION: Stand.
ACTION: Touch right hand to left
shoulder blade behind the head.
Grasp right elbow with left hand and
push GENTLY downwards. Hold for
a count of ten. Repeat nine times.
Repeat stretch sequence touching
left hand to right shoulder blade.

• • • • • • **STRETCH NO. 7**
PURPOSE: Pectorals and biceps.
POSITION: Stand with right side of
body less than a foot from a wall.
Stretch right arm and hand behind
right shoulder. Place right palm
against the wall.
ACTION: Gently lean against wall.
Hold for a count of ten. Repeat nine
times. Repeat stretch sequence with
left arm and hand.

**STRETCH No. 8**
PURPOSE: To stretch neck muscles.
POSITION: Stand with shoulders
down and relaxed, head straight.
ACTION: Slowly lower right ear towards right shoulder. Hold for a
count of three. Return head to starting position. Slowly lower chin
towards chest. Hold for a count of
three. Return head to starting position. Slowly lower left ear towards
left shoulder. Hold for a count of
ten. Return head to starting position.
Repeat stretch sequence nine times.

• • • • • • **STRETCH No. 9**
PURPOSE: To stretch inner thigh muscles.
POSITION: Sit on the ground with the soles of the feet together. Rest elbows on the inside of the knees.
ACTION: Apply gentle pressure downward on knees with the elbows. Hold for a count of ten. Repeat nine times.

**STRETCH No. 10**
PURPOSE: To stretch buttocks and lower back muscles.
POSITION: Sit on ground with right leg over left leg, and left leg straight out. Bend right knee until right foot touches the ground beside the left knee.
ACTION: Place elbow outside the right knee. Turn head to the right. Hold for a count of ten. Repeat nine times. Repeat stretch sequence with the left side.

## • • • • • STRETCH No. 11
PURPOSE: To strengthen abdominal muscles.
POSITION: Lie down with the knees bent and feet on the ground. Place hands behind head, keeping elbows even with the back of the head.
ACTION: Lift head, shoulders and shoulder blades off the ground. Hold for a count of ten. Return to starting position. Repeat nine times.

## STRETCH No. 12

PURPOSE: To stretch the lower back muscles.

POSITION: Lie with head and shoulders on the ground, knees bent, feet flat.

ACTION: Raise right knee. Wrap hands around right calf. Pull right knee to chest. Hold for a count of ten. Repeat nine times. Repeat stretch sequence with left knee.

• • • • • **STRETCH No.13**
PURPOSE: To stretch groin muscle
at the front of the hip.
POSITION: Assume the lunge
position, with the left knee bent
and right leg straight out behind
the buttocks.
ACTION: Lean forward over the left
knee, but not beyond the left foot.
Hold for a count of ten. Repeat nine
times. Repeat sequence with right
knee bent.

### STRETCH No.14

This stretch is a bonus. It will increase the flow of blood throughout the body.

PURPOSE: To provide a general cardio-vascular pre-game warm-up.
POSITION: Stand at home plate.
ACTION: Do your best home-run trot around the bases five times. In mid-season or as your overall conditioning improves, increase to ten times around the bases.

If you can't warm up on the infield, two circuits of the outfield perimeter is usually about 1300 feet depending on the park, the equivalent of five times around the bases.

When — and only when — you're feeling really fit and pleased with yourself, you might imitate the pros by doing wind sprints in the outfield prior to a game.

# The Final Word

• • • • •

Actually, we were going to forego this chapter and just give you a few pages for notes, but who ever writes notes in the backs of books anyway?

The whole idea of writing our little book was to give you an entertaining and informative collection of tips to help you and your teammates play a better and more enjoyable calibre of slo-pitch. Hopefully, it has worked for you. We probably missed a few areas of the game...like league organization, tournament draws, post-game parties and colour-coordinating your uniforms. Hey, we can't do it all in one book.

Besides, there may be room for a *Son of Play Better Slo-Pitch* some day. So send us your tips!

*Photograph by Dave Bonany*

# Acknowledgements

The authors would like to express their sincere appreciation to the special people who donated their time, ideas, experience, encouragement, guidance, laughter, anecdotes, and above all, patience. To the following people and the others who will recognize their input in the content of this book, we offer our utmost thanks.

Gord Ambrose
Bob Shelston
Coleene Wilson
Greg Olson
Steve Rigby
Janice McCann
Rick Gossage
Ann Johnston
Nigel Napier-Andrews
The men and women of the
Unionville Slo-pitch leagues

Printed in Canada